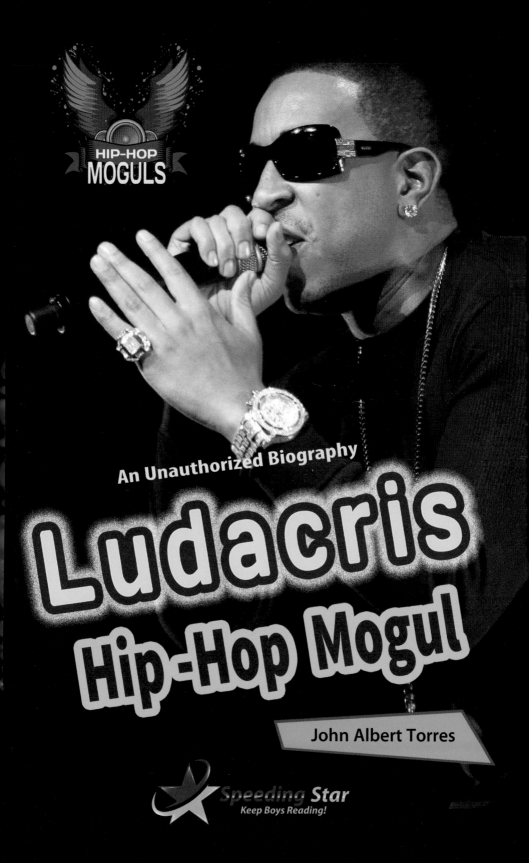

HIP-HOP
MOGULS

An Unauthorized Biography

Ludacris
Hip-Hop Mogul

John Albert Torres

Speeding Star
Keep Boys Reading!

Library of Congress Cataloging-in-Publication Data

Torres, John Albert.
   Ludacris : hip-hop mogul / John Albert Torres.
      pages cm. — (Hip-hop moguls)
   Includes bibliographical references and index.
   Summary: "In this biography of Hip-Hop mogul Ludacris, read everything about him from
     his life-changing internship at a radio station to his rise to fame as a rapper and movie
     star"— Provided by publisher.
   ISBN 978-1-62285-196-6
   1. Ludacris (Rapper)—Juvenile literature. 2. Rap musicians—United States—Biography—
     Juvenile literature. I. Title.
   ML3930.L85T67 2014
   782.421649092—dc23
   [B]   2013048846

Future Editions:
Paperback ISBN: 978-1-62285-197-3   EPUB ISBN: 978-1-62285-198-0
Single-User PDF ISBN: 978-1-62285-199-7   Multi-User PDF: 978-1-62285-200-0

Printed in the United States of America

052014 Lake Book Manufacturing, Inc., Melrose Park, IL

10 9 8 7 6 5 4 3 2 1

To Our Readers: This book has not been authorized by Ludacris or his agents.

We have done our best to make sure all Internet addresses in this book were active and
appropriate when we went to press. However, the author and the Publisher have no control
over, and assume no liability for, the material available on those Internet sites or on other Web
sites they may link to. Any comments or suggestions can be sent by e-mail to comments@
speedingstar.com or to the address below:

Speeding Star
Box 398, 40 Industrial Road
Berkeley Heights, NJ 07922
USA
www.speedingstar.com

♻ Enslow Publishers, Inc., is committed to printing our books on recycled paper. The paper in
every book contains 10% to 30% post-consumer waste (PCW). The cover board on the outside
of each book contains 100% PCW. Our goal is to do our part to help young people and the
environment too!

Contents

ovie fans may have wondered who the new actor was that landed one of the lead roles in *2 Fast 2 Furious,* the second of the wildly popular *Fast and Furious* movie franchise. Music fans might have recognized him right away but were probably still surprised that one of music's most popular rappers, Ludacris, was on the big screen.

His hit single at the time, "Act a Fool," which was on the movie's soundtrack, was getting lots of radio airplay. Many people were familiar

Chapter 1

I Know That Guy

Ludacris is shown with fellow cast member Luke Evans at the premiere of their film *Fast & Furious 6*.

with the video. But it was still a surprise to see him in the movie.

Ludacris played Tej Parker, a former street racer who helped organize car races in the streets. And he did a terrific job, proving that he was a natural actor.

It's not uncommon to see music stars cross over and make an appearance in a movie. But it is uncommon to see someone like Ludacris do it and do it so well. He has appeared in several of the *Fast and Furious* movies, and moviegoers look forward to seeing what kind of trouble Tej Parker will get into next.

Ludacris has proven himself to be a superstar in the music industry and a real presence on the silver screen, while showing no signs of slowing down. In addition to hit records, he continues to act in award-winning films. He is so good at just about everything he tries that he is one of only a few people ever to win a Screen Actors Guild Award, for his work in the highly acclaimed drama *Crash*, as well as a Critic's Choice Award, a Grammy Award, and an MTV Video Music Award.

He has also earned praise for his work on television. Ludacris has appeared in many television programs including *Law & Order: Special Victims Unit*. Not content to stand still, Ludacris is always on the go, trying his hand at new things. He even owns a restaurant that he has an active role in running.

Even though he had achieved popularity on urban and African-American radio stations, it wasn't really until 2003 that Ludacris really made it as more of a

mainstream, or crossover, pop star. That wider stardom is what likely helped him land roles on television and on the silver screen.

His third album was out in 2003 and continued moving up the urban music charts. At the same time, he was also touring with Papa Roach. Some of the more adult and explicit lyrics in his songs were what kept them from being played on the mainstream radio stations or having the videos on MTV. But, with some creative

Ludacris and some of his closest friends arrive at the 2002 MTV Video Music Awards, held at the Radio City Music Hall in New York City.

One of the biggest moments for Ludacris came in 2012 when he performed at the Georgia Dome during halftime of an Atlanta Falcons game. It was special because Atlanta is his hometown.

editing, a song called "Move" became a breakout hit. Ludacris was even invited to sing the song at the 2002 MTV Video Music Awards ceremony with the entire nation watching. His performance that night seemed to change the public's perception, or idea, about Ludacris. It became an important moment in his career. Mainstream success and popularity and movie roles would soon follow.

9

Ludacris knew he wanted to make it in the music industry. But even he couldn't have imagined how big of a star he has become.

Even the popular soda company, Pepsi, used the song "Move," in its commercials and showed Ludacris drinking a soda during the ads. Some people complained that Pepsi should not be using a Ludacris song because many of his songs have very explicit lyrics. Eventually the ads were pulled from airing on television. However, Ludacris was able to keep the money he earned when he originally signed with Pepsi. The song would go on to be recorded and sampled by many other artists including a Puerto Rican group and a hard rock group in the United States. The song even enjoyed a lot of success overseas. It was featured in at least two British television shows over in the United Kingdom.

The future was starting to look really bright for the star born Christopher Brian Bridges. Little did he know that he would soon be starring in movies.

Ludacris is one of those rare people who knew what he wanted to do with his life from a very young age. When he was only nine years old, he already knew that his life would be in music. But what he didn't know though was that it would take a few twists and turns to get there. Those included working as a DJ, selling records out of the trunk of his car, and even studying music management at a university.

Christopher Brian Bridges, who would one day be known around the world as the rapper and actor Ludacris, was born September 11, 1977 in Champaign, Illinois. His parents are Roberta Shields and Wayne Brian Bridges.

Champaign is a small city of about eighty-two thousand people. It is a two-hour drive from both Chicago and Indianapolis and about three hours from St. Louis. It is mainly a quiet city near a lot of farm land. There are two colleges within the city, and more recently the city

Chapter 2

Growing Up

Shown in 2009, Ludacris and his mother Roberta Shields attend a White House Correspondents' Association Dinner in Washington D.C.

has become known for a lot of start-up technology companies.

For Ludacris, it represented a nice, safe place to grow up. From a very young age, he became exposed to music. His parents were very young when he was born. In fact, both of them were still in college at the time of his birth. They would often take their infant baby to listen to house jams and music groups that were performing on campus and in coffee houses.

"They were always jamming to the old school stuff, like Frankie Beverly and Maze, Cameo, all that kind of music," said Ludacris. "They used to take me to college parties and let me get out in the middle of the floor and dance for all the other students."

Even at home, his parents were constantly listening to music. It would set the tone for the rest of his life.

Ludacris and fellow southern rappers T.I. (left) and Young Jeezy (center) are shown at a 2008 election rally supporting Democratic U.S. Senate candidate Jim Martin.

They may come from two entirely different backgrounds and have different styles, but as artists, Ludacris and Jay-Z (left) produce music that hip-hop fans love.

"Man, it was all 'bout music. I used to wakeup everyday listening to music that my parents would put on and that's what got me so interested," he said in an interview with Livewire. "I loved the whole aspect of entertaining. I grew up on James Brown, RUN D.M.C., Fat Boys, ya know?"

It wasn't long before the youngster was drawn to rap music. He enjoyed listening to the rhymes.

"I wrote my first rhyme when I was like nine years old," he said.

He was not only writing rhymes, raps, and lyrics, but he was performing them too. He would sing and rap for anyone who would listen. At first, his audience consisted of only his parents. But soon it began to grow.

15

When he turned twelve years old, Christopher started a hip-hop group among his friends. They called themselves the Loudmouth Hooligans. The group would perform at any venue they could find or at any open-mic event that would allow amateurs to come up and perform a song.

Unfortunately, the band was forced to break up later that same year. Christopher's family decided to move to Atlanta, Georgia. At first he was sad about the move, but he loved Atlanta once he got to know it a little. Plus, Atlanta was, and still is, one of the hotbeds for hip-hop and urban music in the country. Many recording artists have gotten their careers started in the Atlanta region, including André 3000, Outkast, Usher, and Arrested Development.

He was determined to stay involved with his music and try to make it his livelihood. He attended College Park's Banneker High School and made friends right away. He found a lot of kids his age who shared the same dream. They would spend all their free time composing lyrics and rhymes and practicing and perfecting their rapping technique.

Sometimes, he was having so much fun working on his music that he would forget to eat! There were some days where he skipped lunch and dinner. He also found it tough to concentrate on his schoolwork at times.

The most fun he had was at lunchtime. It was there in the cafeteria and outside in the schoolyard that Ludacris and his friends would "battle." These were

From performing in schoolyards to performing at the MTV Video Music Awards with Pharrell Williams, Ludacris has worked his way to the top.

verbal contests where one rapper would try and outdo the next person. Many times the spontaneous lyrics and rhymes were good-natured insults, poking fun at the other person.

It should come to no surprise that Ludacris began to win every single battle. No one his age had the rapping skills he had. People were amazed by what they saw and how well the young rapper sounded.

As a result, he started gaining confidence in his ability to rap, and it wasn't long before he was performing

In 2006, Ludacris went around the country visiting several colleges and universities to raise AIDS awareness.

beyond the school walls. A young Ludacris would show up at talent shows and clubs and do his thing to a tremendous applause that he seemed to feed off of. It made him more determined to succeed and become the music star he always wanted to be.

"I would show up at any venue that had an open mic" he said.

Christopher realized that he wanted to make music his life's work. So he decided to study it in college. He graduated from high school in 1996 and attended Georgia State University. For those few years, he studied music management. This was an important step in his development, and one that you don't hear of often in the rap music genre. The majority of well-known rap stars seemed to share the common experience of tough times and living in rough neighborhoods. Many of them, such as Jay-Z for example, rap about their experiences and how hard it was for them to make it through their youth amid violence and drugs.

Ludacris? He decided to go to college. It was a decision that would change his life. While he was a college student, Christopher came upon an opportunity to do an internship at a local radio station. An internship is where a student is able to work somewhere and learn on-the-job skills. Usually the student is paid in college credits and not with money.

It didn't matter to the student who would soon be known as Ludacris. This internship would impact his life in ways he always dreamed.

The internship led to a permanent job at one of Atlanta's hottest hip-hop stations back then, Hot 97.5. He took over as the producer of the overnight show. The job allowed him to listen to all the latest and hottest rap and hip-hop music. He learned what kinds of beats were the most popular among listeners and what kinds of lyrics and melodies the fans liked, too.

He studied the music and the trends, and he continued writing his lyrics and experimenting with different beats.

Chapter 3

Radio Radio

Because Ludacris is known for being able to rap on so many different types of beats, many big name artists enjoy being able to work with him. Lil Wayne is one example.

This was a very valuable experience. And it also gave him the chance to try out his own rapping style to a much wider audience. He started rapping on voice-over promotions. These are the on-air commercials for the radio station announcing concerts, special events, or other general announcements.

His rapping style was so good and so much fun that he soon became just as popular as the station's most popular radio personalities. He became known on the air as "Chris Lova Lova."

"I started rapping on the station promos. We did them over all of the top hits, so people got to hear me rap over tight beats."

While he loved what he was doing, Ludacris made it no secret that he would rather be a rapper than a producer at a radio station. The problem was that no record companies would give him a deal. But he didn't let that put a damper on his dreams. He decided that he would have keep saving as much money as he could and record his own record.

This was a gamble, but it was a smart gamble. Ludacris already knew so many people now in the Atlanta-area radio markets that he was pretty sure his songs would get played a lot—if they were any good that is!

Lucky for him the songs were good—very good. He named the album *Incognegro*. The first single that he released was called "What's Your Fantasy" It became a pretty big hit on southern hip-hop radio stations. The album sold thirty thousand copies in only three months and the hit song was getting played nearly five hundred times a week on the radio.

That caught the eye of several record companies. Suddenly, the guy who wasn't able to get one record company interested in his work had a few of them bidding for his services. It wouldn't be long before Ludacris could leave his job at the radio station and become the music star he always wanted to be.

Many record company executives made their sales pitches. They took him out to dinner and told him how they would make him a star.

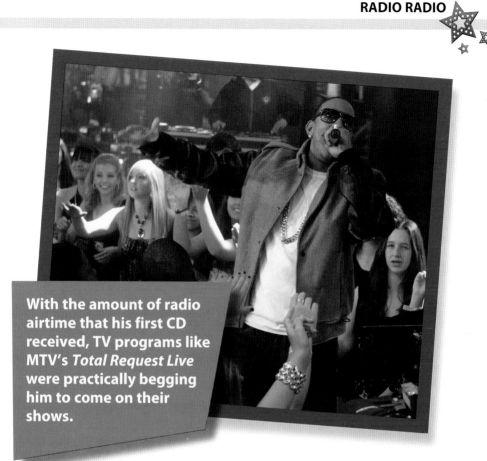

With the amount of radio airtime that his first CD received, TV programs like MTV's *Total Request Live* were practically begging him to come on their shows.

The music personality and record company executive, Brad Jordan, also known as "Scarface," started spending a lot of time with Ludacris, trying to convince him to sign with his record label, Def Jam South. His persistence paid off and before long, Ludacris was the newest artist on the Def Jam label.

Ludacris went right into the studio and started recording new songs. This time, the record would be even more polished and professional than the one he did by himself. He had the backing of a multi-million dollar company. The result was a terrific album of songs with a clever title: *Back for the First Time.*

It was obvious to his listeners that Ludacris was inspired and influenced by many different artists. The album showcased his versatility. He went from smooth to rough to herky-jerky with relative ease, and switched it up from song to song. The beats and rhythms also varied wildly. The album was a smash hit and made it to number four on the *Billboard* 200 chart.

It was also a shrewd idea to include many popular musical artists as guests on the record. Some of the singers and rappers featured included: I-20, Shawnna, Foxy Brown, Pastor Troy, and Timbaland.

"What's Your Fantasy" was re-released on the album and became a true hit single along with the other smash song "Southern Hospitality." Both songs shot up the urban music charts and were getting airplay all over the country.

Ludacris was now a star!

But fans still wanted to know why he called himself "Ludacris." He finally revealed the answer during an interview on MTV. He said the stage name was a combination of his first name, Chris, and the wild and crazy personality that he takes on when he is onstage. He described his actions on stage as "ridiculous and ludicrous." But the fans loved the show. It wasn't just great music, but it was also great entertainment.

"Ludacris—that's how my music is," he exclaimed. "Ludacris means crazy and wild and ridiculous, that is exactly how I would explain it to them. It's looking for a little fun in their lives."

With his wild and outrageous personality, fans know that they will get more than just good music at a Ludacris concert.

Ludacris is shown with the two Grammy Awards that he won in 2007 for Best Rap Album and Best Rap Song.

During another interview, Ludacris revealed the artists that inspired him the most, especially when he was writing his songs and his rhymes. Interestingly, his inspiration comes from outside the music world too!

"I've been influenced by many people, especially the Geto Boys, Uncle Scarface, which is the president of Def Jam. People like 8Ball and Outkast to name a few. A lot of movies influence me. I like to watch comedians for a laugh. I get a lot out of television, and other entertainment has influenced me and my rap style."

That quote provides a strong hint as to how Ludacris has been able to diversify his career so much and make the move from music to movies.

Wisely, Ludacris wanted to capitalize on the success of his first album on the Def Jam label. The only way to do that was to get right back in the studio and record more songs. He didn't want music fans to forget his name. It was important to strike while he was still hot.

He was afraid of being known as a "one-hit wonder."

Ludacris went right back to work writing songs and composing beats. He soon released his follow-up album—*Word of Mouf*—by

Chapter 4

Star Power

At the Los Angeles premiere of *Fast & Furious 6*, Ludacris is shown performing onstage with co-star and fellow musician Tyrese Gibson (left) and co-star Vin Diesel (middle).

the end of 2001. The first single on the record was called "Rollout (My Business)." It became a big hit, and the music video also became very popular. His fans weren't the only ones who loved it. The critics did as well and the video was nominated for a Grammy Award.

A Grammy Award is the highest honor a music star can win. Many great musical artists over the years have gone their entire careers without ever winning a Grammy or even being nominated for one. Finalists for every category are nominated and then the winner is announced during the Grammy Awards ceremony.

It is normally the biggest night of the year for the music industry. Simply being nominated is a special honor.

Ludacris used the same recipe on *Word of Mouf* that he did for his first record. He brought in a lot of well-known rappers and singers to appear on his record. He released singles that featured artists such as Nate Dogg, Sleepy Brown, and Mystikal.

The album did very well. In fact, it hit No. 3 on the *Billboard* music charts the very week it was released. On this recording, Ludacris really revealed his funny side. The lyrics and raps are sharp, witty and even downright funny. One music critic called it a great combination of a music album and a comedy album.

"Whether he's delivering a punchy one-liner, exaggerating his rhyme flow to a silly extreme or cleverly deploying pop culture references, Ludacris keeps the mood light and festive," wrote Soren Baker of the *Chicago Tribune*. "Even his skits are funny enough that they could serve as the foundation for a top-tier comedy album."

While the album peaked at number three on the pop charts, it hit the number one slot on *Billboard*'s Rap Albums chart!

Ludacris was now considered a star. Nope, he was no longer in danger of being a one-hit wonder. Unafraid that his fans would forget him now, the tireless worker decided to take a short break.

He returned to work after a few months by releasing a new single. It was called "Act a Fool" and it was from the *2 Fast 2 Furious* soundtrack. The song enjoyed some success but was not a monster hit. Pretty soon after that, Ludacris released his newest album, a southern-styled rap album called *Chicken-n-Beer*.

The album shot up to No. 1 on the *Billboard* pop charts the very first week it was released.

Once again, the album featured comedy elements and lots of jokes and skits. But this time around, many of the jokes were of an adult nature and that may have limited the audience a bit. Some listeners didn't like the type of joking that was going on in many of the songs. For the first time, critics disagreed on whether they enjoyed the record.

One critic called it "cartoonish," while another said that too many of the songs felt like one-note jokes stretched out to three or four minutes. But another critic described the music as simply a lot of fun and full of glee.

Again, the album featured many guest hip-hop artists, including Snoop Dogg and Chingy, among others.

In a 2003 interview with *Livewire*, Ludacris admitted that he was trying to push the limits on his record and try something new.

"My rap is always moving in a new direction and it always will be," he said. "You have to satisfy the core audience that I have and then move on and show my progression and growth also. There is always going to be growth. I'm going to grow each and every day and learn more and, you know, grow as an individual and so will my music. Music changes each and every day."

His music was soon on television, featured on Pepsi-Cola television ads.

After a few weeks on the charts, album sales fell significantly. This was due, in part to there being no real hit single on the record. That is, until one of the songs, "Stand Up," was also featured in a teen hip-hop movie called *You Got Served*. At the time, this was the biggest mainstream hit of the rapper's young career.

Ludacris and Chingy are shown performing at the filming of their music video for the song "Gimme Dat."

The song shot up to the number one position on *Billboard*'s Top 100. It received airplay on all types of radio stations from hip-hop and urban, to mainstream pop, to MTV. The album was eventually nominated for a Grammy Award, however, did not win.

"I can't say that I'm not disappointed," he told *Livewire* afterward. "I tell you I'm happy to have been nominated for the Grammy because there's a lot of extra publicity and press *just* being nominated. So, ya know, I'm very happy just to have been nominated."

But he did win the first of three Grammy Awards later on. Ludacris received his first after combining with Usher and Lil Jon on the hit single "Yeah!"

The funny and outspoken rapper also received a lot of extra press and publicity when he became involved in a war of words with conservative talk show host Bill O'Reilly, who criticized the rapper for being a poor role model for young people. O'Reilly also criticized Pepsi for hiring Ludacris to promote its products.

Ludacris responded to O'Reilly and his other critics in a very harsh, dark, and gritty song and music video that was very different from the funny and colorful songs that his fans were accustomed to.

The song was called "Blow It Out," and the rapper even mentions O'Reilly by name. While it wasn't one of his finer moments, Ludacris made sure he got his message across to Mr. O'Reilly.

Ludacris didn't have to do a whole lot of acting when he landed his first big movie role in *2 Fast 2 Furious*. The character he plays, Tej Parker, is a wisecracking funny guy who brings some comic relief to a movie filled with intense car chases.

Hmm, funny guy? Yep, that sounds like Ludacris. He sort of just acts like himself in the film. But he was so good in the 2003 movie that he was invited to audition for a big Hollywood film about racism in America

Chapter 5

Movie Star

called *Crash*. The entire movie takes place over a thirty-six-hour period in which several stories intertwine.

He had long admired actor Don Cheadle and was thrilled to see that Cheadle was one of the producers on the film.

"I went for an audition for Crash and next thing I knew, I had it," Ludacris told MTV during an interview.

Playing a thief in the movie *Crash*, Ludacris had to really do some acting. It was the first time in his life he would have to say things he didn't personally believe in and act in a way that wasn't him. That's why they call it acting.

He was very good in the film, which went on to be a smash hit. It won an Academy Award, known as the Oscar, for best film of the year! When he arrived on the set, Ludacris said it was a little intimidating to see so many great actors like Sandra Bullock, Don Cheadle, and Matt Dillon. He decided the only way for this to work would be to act like a student and try to learn everything he could about acting from the others.

One of his fellow actors, perhaps seeing that he was nervous, gave him some good advice. He told Ludacris to just be himself and have fun with the role. Ludacris said that he knew the film was going to be something special while he was working on it, but he was amazed when he sat in the theater and saw the finished product for the first time.

"It feels great to be in an Oscar winning movie," he told MTV. "I definitely knew I was going to get one eventually. I just didn't think it would happen this soon in my life."

He also was awarded a Critic's Choice Award.

After his performance in *Crash*, the acting offers started rolling in. Everyone wanted his acting, voice, or face to be part of their program. Pretty soon he was on television shows like *The Simpsons* and *Law & Order*, and even as a voice on video games like *Madden* football.

From left to right, Ludacris is shown with fellow cast members Matt Dillon, Don Cheadle, Terrence Howard, and Larenz Tate of the film *Crash*. They are holding their trophies for Outstanding Performance by a Cast at the Screen Actors Guild Awards.

Ludacris and his foundation have given back to the community in a number of ways. This includes partnering with Nissan to give away twenty cars to selected families in the Atlanta area.

But he also kept popping up on the big screen. He played the funny, music-loving elf DJ Donnie in *Fred Claus*. He played Brendan in the romantic holiday movie *New Year's Eve*, and the character Skinny Black in *Hustle & Flow*.

And, of course, he continued appearing as Tej Parker in the *Fast and Furious* movies.

Most successful musical artists who then went on to become award-winning actors would barely have time for anything else. But Ludacris is different. In addition to being a music star and acting star, he found enough time to help others in need.

He started the Ludacris Foundation early in his career. The foundation's goal is to inspire middle-school aged children to be the best they can be by using the arts and music. *Black Enterprise* magazine named the Ludacris Foundation as one of the Top 20 Leading Philanthropy Foundations.

The foundation stresses leadership, education, and living a healthy lifestyle. Ludacris and his foundation have helped thousands of at-risk kids over the years.

In 2011 he also got involved with the organization Dosomething.org to help buy books to fill the libraries of New Orleans, Louisiana. Many of the libraries in New Orleans were damaged following the flooding brought on by Hurricane Katrina.

He was also recently honored for his work in raising awareness for diabetes. He has also lent his name, his time, his music, and his efforts to the following charities:

Artists for Peace and Justice; Charity Folks; Common Ground Foundation; Get Schooled Foundation; Grammy Foundation; Live Earth; MusiCares; The Black Eyed Peas Foundation; and Thorn.

Around Thanksgiving every year, Ludacris teams up with his foundation and some area restaurants to serve holiday meals to the homeless. They also give out thousands of turkeys to the community.

According to a Web site that keeps track of which celebrities are most charitable, Ludacris was listed as being involved with eleven charities and helping nearly twenty causes.

While all this is going on, Ludacris is well aware that what made him famous was his rapping. Even while he was making movies and handing out turkeys, he was also in the recording studio working on his latest record.

udacris stopped joking around so much on his next two albums *The Red Light District* and *Release Therapy*. He started singing about more mature themes and even dabbled in some political stuff, too.

To help promote both albums he appeared and performed on *Saturday Night Live (SNL)*, a late-night music and comedy show that is aired live.

Ludacris continued recording more adult music over the next few years and

chapter 6

Music and More Music

enjoyed chart success and good radio play with the release of *Theater of the Mind* in 2008 and *Battle of the Sexes* in 2010. Over the years, he continued to record with other well-known artists on his recordings. He even featured stars like Lil Wayne and Kanye West.

It took Ludacris a little longer to come out with his next album, his eighth. In fact, maybe to clear his

After having a much talked about feud, Ludacris and fellow Southern rapper T.I. put aside their differences in 2008. They have since collaborated on several songs.

Even though the release of his newest album is taking longer than expected, it doesn't stop Ludacris from performing at large venues like the Bonnaroo Music and Arts Festival in Manchester, Tennessee.

Ludacris has definitely stayed active while the world anxiously awaits the release of his album *Ludaversal*. He's shown performing at the opening party of O1NE Yas Island nightclub in Abu Dhabi.

head or just get some fresh ideas, the rapper decided to record his next album, *Ludaversal*, in France. He enlisted superstar Chris Brown to do a song with him and flew his friend out to France, where they were spotted partying all over Paris.

Ludacris is not too open about his personal life and what happens away from the stage. We do know that he has two daughters with two separate women, though he is not married.

We also know that one of the main reasons he became involved as a spokesman for diabetes was because the terrible disease claimed his father's life in 2007. His father's disease was brought on by alcoholism, a topic that Ludacris tackles in a song about his father rumored to be on his long-awaited *Ludaversal* album. The song is called "Ocean Skies."

"It was really talking about my father and alcoholism and me losing him," he told *Vibe* magazine in an interview. "That is basically what the song is about. Like I said, talking about being vulnerable and my personal life, that's really what this album is. That song is about growing up and trying to get him to stop [drinking] and me dealing with that."

While recording in France, Ludacris fell in love with an African medical student studying in France. Many reports say the couple is engaged to be married, though Ludacris would not confirm it.

"I try to preserve certain things and keep things special, and that is one thing that I would like to keep private," he told reporters in France.

Whether it was due to creative difficulties or just the fact that he was spending so much time with his new girlfriend, the *Ludaversal* album had to be delayed several times. But not wanting to keep his fans waiting for too long, Ludacris started releasing new songs on Fridays through the internet. These digital singles have represented some of his best work and some have become very popular.

The best thing, for fans anyway, is that the songs were free.

"You know, we shot five movies over the past three years, so after the ten-year anniversary I felt like it was time to give people a little bit of a break from Ludacris in terms of the music scene so I shot some movies, and now we back to the music and the grind right now," he said during a radio interview in 2013.

He also said, during the same radio interview, that the album, has taken him longer than normal because he's been experimenting with new sounds and techniques.

"In terms of experimentation, I think every artist experiments on their album," he said. "It's just the amount of experimentation, and you just keepin' in true to your roots. So me, I'm keepin' it true to my roots, but I feel like everything needs to be evolution, there needs to be progression, from every single album, so that's what I continue to do."

Discography

Incognegro, 1999

Back for the First Time, 2000

Word of Mouf, 2001

Chicken-n-Beer, 2003

The Red Light District, 2004

Release Therapy, 2006

Theater of the Mind, 2008

Battle of the Sexes, 2010

Ludaversal, 2014**(Release date not confirmed yet)

Internet Addresses

LUDACRIS'S DEF JAM PAGE
http://www.defjam.com/artists/ludacris/
OFFICIAL TWITTER PAGE
https://twitter.com/Ludacris

2004   Hot 100 Single of the Year (with Usher and Lil Jon), *Billboard* Music Awards

Mainstream Top 40 Single of the Year (with Usher and Lil Jon), *Billboard* Music Awards

Male Artist of the Year, *Source* Awards

R&B/Rap Collaboration (with Usher and Lil Jon), Source Awards

2005   Rap Song of the Year (with Lil Jon & the Eastside Boyz and Usher), *Billboard* Music Awards

Best Dirty in the Movie, Dirty Awards

Crunkest Crib, Dirty Awards

Dirty Humanitarian Award (shared with David Banner), Dirty Awards

Best Rap/Sung Collaboration (with Usher and Lil Jon), Grammy Awards

Best Rap Video, MTV Video Music Awards

Best R&B/Soul or Rap Dance Cut (with Usher and Lil Jon), Soul Train Music Awards

Coolest Collabo (with Ciara), Vibe Awards

Video Goddess (for Esther Baxter), *Vibe* Awards

2006   Outstanding Performance by a Cast in a Motion Picture (with Sandra Bullock, Brendan Fraser, and Thandie Newton), Screen Actors Guild Awards

2007   Best Collaboration (with Mary J. Blige), BET Awards

Best Rap Album, Grammy Awards

Best Rap Song (with Pharrell Williams), Grammy Awards

Index